W9-CBI-249

First edition for the United States, its territories and dependencies, the Philippines, and Canada published in 2006 by Barron's Educational Series, Inc.

First edition for Great Britain published 2006 by Hodder Children's Books, a division of Hodder Headline Limited.



*All inquiries should be addressed to:*
Barron's Educational Series, Inc.
250 Wireless Boulevard
Hauppauge, New York 11788
***http://www.barronseduc.com***

Library of Congress Catalog Card No. 2004116974

ISBN-13: 978-0-7641-3214-8
ISBN-10: 0-7641-3214-8

Printed in China
9 8 7 6 5 4 3 2 1

# I'm Telling the Truth

A FIRST LOOK AT HONESTY

PAT THOMAS
ILLUSTRATED BY LESLEY HARKER

If someone told you that the sky was yellow
or that frogs had wings you would know
that they weren't telling the truth.

Most of us know the difference between what is true and what isn't. And most of us know how important it is to tell the truth.

There are lots of reasons why people aren't honest. Sometimes it's because they feel ashamed, or they want to impress others.

Some people say things that aren't true to get things that they want but don't really deserve.

## What about you?

Can you think of someone you know about – it could be someone in a story or a real person – who isn't honest? What sorts of things happened to them?

Being honest takes a lot of practice.

It isn't always easy to find a polite way to tell the truth that doesn't hurt other people's feelings.

Remember that the people who love you the most will always be happy that you told them the truth, even if it's not what they hoped you would say.

But sometimes if you can't find something nice to say, it's best not to say anything at all.

Often people tell lies when they are afraid of getting into trouble.

But lying only makes you feel bad about yourself.

When you haven't been honest it can make you feel worried and anxious that someone will find out.

Telling the truth helps you to feel good about yourself.

Learning to be honest helps you feel confident and brave.

And you usually get into less trouble for telling the truth than you do for lying – and getting caught.

Sometimes it's not what
you say but the way
you act that counts.

One good way to
be honest is to never
take things that
don't belong
to you.

It's also important to keep your word.

If you say you are going to do something,
make sure you do it.

You can also show how honest you can be by speaking up when you see something wrong...

…and letting others know your true thoughts and feelings.

Even though being honest can be hard sometimes, it is worth it.

Telling the truth lets everyone know what really happened.

It helps us avoid misunderstandings and keeps innocent people from being blamed or punished.

## What about you?

Have you ever been blamed for something you didn't do? Was there someone who could have helped you by telling the truth?

People who don't practice being honest slowly lose all their friends.

This is because friends need to be able to trust one another.

Nobody can trust a person who acts dishonestly or says things that are not true.

Everyone likes to be around people who speak the truth and keep their word.

When we all practice being honest, the world becomes a fairer and happier place to live in.

# HOW TO USE THIS BOOK

Teaching honesty and responsibility takes a considerable amount of time and patience. It isn't anything like teaching children how to tie their shoes, where they pick up the basic concept after a few lessons. Instead, we need to look for ways to nurture within our children a desire to do the right thing, to value honesty, to say what's on their minds, and to act with integrity and good will.

We teach our children honesty by being honest ourselves. Avoid lying to your child, even about difficult subjects such as illness, death, or divorce. It's better to admit that some things are hard to talk about than to try to cover them up. It's also OK to let your children see you struggling with issues of integrity and honesty.

Praise your child when he or she is acting in an honest and responsible way. When you are watching TV or reading books, take the opportunity to point out and discuss examples of honest behavior. Use the "What about you?" prompts in this book to discuss with your child examples of honesty and the consequences of dishonesty.

If your child is telling lies or behaving in a dishonest way, find out why. The major reasons children lie are to escape punishment and to get away with the forbidden. Chances are the harsher your punishing, the more motivated the child will be to avoid owning up when he or she does wrong. Where possible, allow the natural consequences of his actions to unfold for your child. If, for instance, he takes something from a store without paying, have him be the one to return it and confront the store manager.

Schools with honor codes and teachers who talk openly about cheating have lower incidences of academic dishonesty. In class, teachers and children can brainstorm all the excuses and rationalizations people give for lying, cheating, and stealing, and then have a discussion about them. How valid are they? What's wrong with each of them? What are the better alternatives?

Children learning about telling the truth often go through a phase of tattling. Busy parents and teachers can find this frustrating. Yet tattling – and the way adults respond to it – begins the process of discrimination and self-sufficiency. If the tattling behavior is dealt with appropriately, adults can empower "tattling" children to begin to solve their problems themselves without running to an outside authority for every little thing.

## BOOKS TO READ

***It Wasn't Me*** (Small Books)
Brian Moses, Mike Gordon (Santillana USA, 1999)

***Oh, Bother! Someone's Fibbing!***
Betty Birney, Sue Dicicco (Golden Press, 1991)

***The Boy Who Cried Wolf***
Tony Ross (Puffin, 1991)

***Pinocchio****
Carlo Collodi, Cooper Edens (Chronicle, 2001)

***Don't Tell a Whopper on Fridays***
Adolph Moser, David Melton (Landmark Editions, 1999)

* Your school or library may have an abridged version of this classic book that is suitable for young children.

## RESOURCES FOR PARENTS

***The Values Book: Teaching Sixteen Basic Values to Young Children***
Pam Schiller, Tamera Bryant (Gryphon House, 1998)

***Teaching Your Children Values***
Linda and Richard Eyre (Fireside, 1993)

***Telling Isn't Tattling***
Kathryn Hammerseng and Dave Garbot (Parenting Press, 1995)

***10-Minute Life Lessons for Kids***
(Perennial, 1998)

***www.goodcharacter.com***
A 2004 Parent's Choice recommendation, this site provides free resources, materials, and lesson plans.